Cooking Thanksgiving Dinner

by
Michèle Dufresne

Pioneer Valley Educational Press, Inc.

Dad, Mom, Nick, and Matt went to the cousins' for Thanksgiving. Grandma and Grandpa went, too.

"We will all help cook," said Grandma. "Here are the potatoes."

"We will cook the potatoes," said the little cousins.

"Oh, no," said Nick. "You are too little!"

"Here are the carrots," said Mom.

"We will cook the carrots," said the little cousins.

"Oh, no," said Matt. "You are too little."

"We are not too little,"
said the little cousins.

"Here is the turkey," said Grandma.

"We will cook the turkey," said the little cousins.

"Oh, no!" said Nick and Matt.

"Oh, yes," said Grandma.
"You can cook the turkey.
I will help."

"This is a great turkey," said Nick and Matt.

"We cooked the turkey!" said the little cousins.